UNDERSTANDING ANXIETY DISORDERS

Comprehensive Guide To Identifying Symptoms, Effective Treatments, Coping Strategies, And Professional Help For Managing Panic Attacks

DR. LINCOLN WAYLON

DISCLAIMER

This book contains information that should only be used for educational and informational reasons; it is not meant to be used as a source of medical or psychological advice. The author's studies, life experiences, and expertise in the area of health and wellness served as the foundation for the content. It should not, however, be used in place of expert counsel, a diagnosis, or medical care.

Any queries you may have about a physical or mental health issue should always be directed toward the advice of a licensed healthcare provider or mental health specialist. With regard to the efficacy or outcomes of the methods or suggestions included in this book, the author and publisher make no representations or warranties.

Any information or methods in this book are used entirely at the reader's own risk and discretion. The material provided here may be used or misused, and neither the author nor the publisher will be held responsible for any results, losses, or negative impacts.

Keep in mind that everyone has different demands and reactions to health and wellness routines. Any health and wellness plans you implement must be customized to your particular circumstances, and you should speak with experts to make sure the plans meet your needs.

TABLE OF CONTENTS

ABOUT THE BOOK

"Understanding Anxiety Disorders" serves as an essential guide to navigating the complex and often challenging world of anxiety-related conditions. By offering a thorough overview of various anxiety disorders, this book provides a comprehensive examination of their definition, historical evolution, and impact on daily life. With a focus on the importance of recognizing and understanding these disorders, it emphasizes the profound effect anxiety can have on individuals and underscores the necessity of effective intervention and support.

The book delves deeply into specific anxiety disorders, beginning with Generalized Anxiety Disorder (GAD), detailing its symptoms, diagnostic criteria, and the common triggers and risk factors associated with it. It offers a broad spectrum of treatment approaches and coping strategies, enriched with case studies and real-life examples that illustrate how these strategies can be applied in practical settings.

Panic Disorder is explored with a detailed look at the nature of panic attacks, their diagnostic criteria, and the various treatment options available. The text also provides valuable self-help techniques and strategies for managing triggers; ensuring readers have a toolkit to handle panic-related challenges effectively.

Social Anxiety Disorder is addressed with an emphasis on understanding social anxiety, its key symptoms, and diagnostic criteria. The book presents effective treatments and practical tips for daily life, including social skills training, to help individuals navigate social situations with greater ease and confidence.

Specific Phobias are examined with a focus on the different types, diagnostic criteria, and the benefits of exposure therapy. Self-help strategies and real-life experiences are included to illustrate how individuals can confront and manage their phobias effectively.

Obsessive-Compulsive Disorder (OCD) is thoroughly explained, highlighting common obsessions and compulsions and exploring various treatment options, including Cognitive Behavioral Therapy (CBT). Personal stories and examples provide a relatable context for understanding how OCD affects individuals and how they can work towards managing it.

The book also delves into the causes and risk factors of anxiety disorders, examining genetic, biological, environmental, and psychological influences. It discusses the impact of stress and trauma and offers preventive measures to mitigate the onset of anxiety disorders.

In the section on diagnosis and assessment, readers will find detailed information on diagnostic tools and techniques, the role of mental health professionals, and the risks of self-diagnosis. Accurate assessment is emphasized as crucial for effective treatment.

Treatment approaches are covered extensively, including Cognitive Behavioral Therapy (CBT), medication options, lifestyle adjustments, and complementary therapies. The book guides managing treatment progress to ensure that readers are well-informed about their options and how to effectively manage their anxiety.

Coping strategies and self-help techniques are thoroughly discussed, offering daily coping techniques, resilience-building exercises, mindfulness and relaxation practices, and insights into support systems and resources. This section is designed to help readers develop long-term strategies for managing anxiety and improving their quality of life.

The book addresses common concerns and frequently asked questions about anxiety disorders, such as distinguishing between normal anxiety and a disorder, initial steps for seeking help, the duration of treatment, and effective self-help strategies. This comprehensive approach ensures that readers are equipped with the knowledge and tools needed to understand and manage anxiety disorders effectively.

CHAPTER ONE

OVERVIEW OF ANXIETY DISORDERS

DEFINITION AND OVERVIEW

Anxiety disorders encompass a range of mental health conditions characterized by excessive worry, fear, or apprehension. They are more than just occasional feelings of nervousness; they involve persistent and overwhelming anxiety that can interfere with daily functioning.

Generalized Anxiety Disorder (GAD), Panic Disorder, Social Anxiety Disorder, and Specific Phobias are some examples. Each disorder has its distinct features but shares the common thread of intense, often irrational, anxiety that disrupts normal life.

Understanding anxiety disorders requires recognizing that they are not just psychological but also physiological. Symptoms can manifest as physical reactions like a rapid heartbeat, sweating, or trembling, alongside mental symptoms such as racing thoughts or persistent fear. These disorders can cause significant distress and impact a person's ability to lead a normal life, making it crucial to identify and address them appropriately.

Diagnosis typically involves a comprehensive evaluation by a mental health professional, including a detailed history and assessment of symptoms. Treatment options vary and may include therapy, medication, or a combination of both. Early intervention can significantly improve outcomes, so recognizing the signs and seeking help is essential.

HISTORICAL PERSPECTIVE

The understanding of anxiety disorders has evolved significantly over time. In ancient times, what we now recognize as anxiety disorders were often attributed to supernatural forces or moral failings.

It wasn't until the 19th and early 20th centuries that medical and psychological perspectives began to emerge. Influential figures like Sigmund Freud contributed to early theories, linking anxiety to unresolved internal conflicts and unconscious processes.

The mid-20th century marked a significant shift with the development of behavioral and cognitive theories, which offered more concrete explanations for anxiety. The introduction of cognitive-behavioral therapy (CBT) revolutionized treatment by focusing on changing dysfunctional thought patterns and behaviors. This period also saw the first medications specifically developed to treat anxiety disorders, such as benzodiazepines and antidepressants.

Today, the understanding of anxiety disorders incorporates biological, psychological, and social factors. Advances in neuroscience and genetics have provided deeper insights into the neurobiological underpinnings of these conditions, leading to more targeted and effective treatments. The ongoing research continues to refine our understanding and improve approaches to managing anxiety disorders.

Common symptoms of anxiety disorders include both psychological and physical manifestations. Psychologically, individuals may experience excessive worry, fear of specific situations or objects, and persistent thoughts about potential threats. These feelings are often disproportionate to the actual risk or danger, causing significant distress and impairing daily activities.

Physically, anxiety can trigger symptoms such as a racing heart, muscle tension, headaches, and gastrointestinal issues. Individuals might also experience sweating, trembling, or dizziness. Panic attacks, characterized by sudden and intense fear, can include symptoms like chest pain, shortness of breath, and a sense of impending doom. Recognizing these symptoms is crucial for seeking appropriate help and treatment.

Behavioral changes are also common, such as avoiding certain situations or places that provoke anxiety. This avoidance can limit personal and professional opportunities, affecting overall quality of life. Addressing these symptoms through therapy or medication can help individuals manage their anxiety and improve their ability to function effectively in daily life.

IMPACT ON DAILY LIFE

Anxiety disorders can significantly impact daily life, affecting various aspects such as work, relationships, and overall well-being. Individuals may find it challenging to perform at work due to concentration issues, excessive worry about performance, or avoidance of certain tasks. This can lead to decreased productivity, job dissatisfaction, and even absenteeism.

Social interactions can also be severely affected. People with anxiety disorders might withdraw from social activities, fearing judgment or embarrassment. This withdrawal can strain relationships with family and friends, leading to feelings of isolation and loneliness. In severe cases, individuals might avoid leaving their homes altogether, impacting their ability to engage in everyday activities.

Overall, anxiety disorders can lead to a diminished quality of life. The constant state of worry and fear can hinder personal growth, limit opportunities, and reduce overall life satisfaction.

Addressing these impacts through effective treatment and support is vital for improving daily functioning and enhancing overall well-being.

IMPORTANCE OF UNDERSTANDING ANXIETY DISORDERS

Understanding anxiety disorders is crucial for several reasons. It fosters empathy and reduces stigma, helping individuals feel more comfortable seeking help and discussing their experiences.

Awareness can also lead to earlier identification and intervention, which is essential for effective treatment and management of the disorder.

Educating oneself about anxiety disorders can also improve communication and support for those affected. Families, friends, and colleagues who understand the challenges of anxiety can offer better support and accommodations. This understanding can also drive policy changes and improve access to mental health resources and treatments.

Furthermore, knowledge about anxiety disorders can empower individuals to recognize symptoms in themselves or others, facilitating timely and appropriate care. It encourages a proactive approach to mental health, promoting strategies for prevention, self-care, and effective management of anxiety disorders.

CHAPTER TWO

PANIC DISORDER

UNDERSTANDING PANIC ATTACKS

Panic attacks are sudden, intense episodes of fear that occur without warning and can peak within minutes. They are characterized by a range of physical and psychological symptoms, including rapid heartbeat, sweating, trembling, shortness of breath, chest pain, dizziness, and a sense of impending doom.

During a panic attack, the bodies "fight or flight" response is triggered, causing a surge of adrenaline that leads to these overwhelming sensations. Recognizing the signs of a panic attack is crucial for understanding the disorder and seeking appropriate help.

The experience of a panic attack can be frightening, often leading individuals to believe they are having a heart attack or losing control. Symptoms can mimic those of other medical conditions, making it essential to differentiate between panic attacks and other potential health issues. A panic attack typically resolves within 20 to 30 minutes, but the fear of experiencing another attack can lead to persistent anxiety and avoidance behaviors, which may worsen the condition over time.

To effectively manage panic attacks, it's important to learn about their triggers and develop strategies to cope with them. Understanding the nature of panic attacks helps individuals recognize when they are occurring and seek appropriate interventions. Regularly practicing relaxation techniques and engaging in cognitive-behavioral strategies can assist in reducing the frequency and severity of panic attacks, contributing to a better quality of life.

DIAGNOSTIC CRITERIA

The diagnosis of panic disorder is based on specific criteria outlined in the Diagnostic and Statistical Manual of Mental Disorders (DSM-5). To meet the criteria for panic disorder, an individual must experience recurrent and unexpected panic attacks along with at least one month of persistent concern about having additional attacks or the consequences of the attacks. The panic attacks must not be attributed to another medical condition or substance use and must cause significant distress or impairment in daily functioning.

A comprehensive evaluation by a mental health professional is essential for an accurate diagnosis. This typically involves a detailed clinical interview where the individual's symptoms, history, and functional impact are assessed.

The clinician may also use standardized assessment tools to measure the frequency and severity of panic attacks, helping to determine if the symptoms meet the criteria for panic disorder or if another anxiety disorder might be present.

Diagnostic criteria help differentiate panic disorder from other conditions with similar symptoms, such as generalized anxiety disorder or specific phobias.

Accurate diagnosis is critical for developing an effective treatment plan tailored to the individual's needs, as different disorders may require different therapeutic approaches. Proper diagnosis ensures that the individual receives the most appropriate and effective care for their specific condition.

TREATMENT OPTIONS

Treatment for panic disorder often includes a combination of psychotherapy, medication, and lifestyle changes. Cognitive-behavioral therapy (CBT) is a highly effective approach that helps individuals understand and change the thought patterns and behaviors that contribute to panic attacks. CBT typically involves exposure to feared situations and teaching coping strategies to manage anxiety. This therapy aims to reduce the frequency and intensity of panic attacks and improve overall functioning.

Medications such as selective serotonin reuptake inhibitors (SSRIs) or benzodiazepines may be prescribed to help manage symptoms. SSRIs help regulate mood and reduce anxiety over time, while benzodiazepines can provide short-term relief from acute anxiety. It's essential to work closely with a healthcare provider to find the right medication and dosage, as individual responses can vary. Medications should be combined with therapy for optimal results.

Lifestyle changes can also play a significant role in managing panic disorder. Regular physical activity, healthy eating, and adequate sleep contribute to overall well-being and can reduce the frequency of panic attacks.

Learning stress management techniques, such as mindfulness and relaxation exercises, can further enhance treatment outcomes. Combining these approaches provides a comprehensive strategy for managing panic disorder effectively.

SELF-HELP TECHNIQUES

Self-help techniques are valuable for managing panic disorder and complement professional treatment.

Deep breathing exercises can help calm the nervous system and reduce the physical symptoms of panic attacks. Practicing deep breathing involves inhaling slowly through the nose, holding the breath for a few seconds, and then exhaling slowly through the mouth. This technique helps counteract the hyperventilation associated with panic attacks and promotes relaxation.

Another effective self-help technique is progressive muscle relaxation, which involves tensing and then slowly relaxing different muscle groups in the body. This practice helps individuals become more aware of physical tension and learn how to release it, reducing overall anxiety. Incorporating mindfulness meditation into daily routines can also help individuals stay present and manage anxious thoughts more effectively.

Keeping a journal to track panic attacks and their triggers can provide valuable insights into patterns and contributing factors. This information can be used to develop personalized coping strategies and discuss them with a therapist during sessions. By actively engaging in self-help techniques and monitoring progress, individuals can take an active role in managing their panic disorder and improving their quality of life.

MANAGING TRIGGERS

Managing triggers is a crucial aspect of coping with panic disorder. Identifying specific situations, stressors, or internal cues that precipitate panic attacks is the first step. Common triggers include high-stress situations, certain environments, or physical sensations like rapid heartbeat. Keeping a detailed record of when panic attacks occur and what factors might have contributed can help in recognizing patterns and developing strategies to address them.

Once triggers are identified, individuals can work on implementing strategies to reduce their impact. This might involve gradually exposing oneself to feared situations in a controlled manner, known as exposure therapy, to build tolerance and reduce fear. Developing coping skills, such as relaxation techniques or cognitive restructuring, can help manage anxiety when faced with triggers. It is also helpful to create a personalized plan for dealing with specific triggers and practicing it regularly.

Avoiding or modifying exposure to known triggers can also be beneficial. For example, if certain activities or situations consistently lead to panic attacks, finding alternative ways to handle them or reducing their frequency can help minimize their impact. By actively managing triggers and implementing coping strategies, individuals can reduce the likelihood of experiencing panic attacks and enhance their overall sense of control and well-being.

CHAPTER THREE

SOCIAL ANXIETY DISORDER

OVERVIEW OF SOCIAL ANXIETY

Social anxiety disorder (SAD) is a prevalent mental health condition characterized by intense fear or anxiety in social situations. Individuals with SAD often experience overwhelming apprehension about being scrutinized or judged by others, which can significantly impair their ability to interact comfortably. This condition goes beyond simple shyness; it involves a persistent and excessive fear that is disproportionate to the actual situation, leading to considerable distress and avoidance behavior. Social anxiety typically manifests during adolescence or early adulthood but can develop at any age.

The fear associated with social anxiety disorder is not limited to specific situations but can be widespread, affecting various social interactions such as public speaking, attending parties, or even engaging in casual conversations. Individuals may worry excessively about embarrassing themselves or being negatively evaluated, which can lead to avoidance of these situations altogether.

As a result, social anxiety can restrict a person's social life and professional opportunities, making it crucial to understand and address the condition effectively.

Managing social anxiety requires a comprehensive understanding of its impact on daily life. This includes recognizing the avoidance patterns and their consequences on personal and professional growth. Early intervention and support are essential for individuals to develop coping strategies and overcome the limitations imposed by their anxiety.

KEY SYMPTOMS AND DIAGNOSTIC CRITERIA

Key symptoms of social anxiety disorder include a marked fear of social or performance situations where one is exposed to possible scrutiny by others. This fear is often accompanied by physical symptoms such as sweating, trembling, or a racing heart, and may lead to a significant impact on daily functioning. To be diagnosed with SAD, the anxiety must be persistent, typically lasting for six months or more, and it should interfere with various aspects of life, including work, school, or social relationships.

Diagnostic criteria for social anxiety disorder include experiencing anxiety in one or more social situations, where the individual fears that they will act in a way that will be humiliating or embarrassing. The anxiety experienced must be out of proportion to the actual threat posed by the social situation and should cause significant distress or impairment in functioning. Diagnosis is usually made through clinical interviews and self-reported questionnaires, which help assess the severity and impact of the symptoms.

Understanding these criteria is crucial for distinguishing social anxiety from other mental health conditions. Accurate diagnosis ensures that individuals receive appropriate treatment and support tailored to their specific needs, facilitating better management of their symptoms and improvement in their overall quality of life.

EFFECTIVE TREATMENTS

Effective treatments for social anxiety disorder often involve a combination of psychotherapy and medication. Cognitive-behavioral therapy (CBT) is a widely recognized and effective form of psychotherapy that helps individuals identify and challenge negative thought patterns and behaviors associated with their anxiety. CBT focuses on gradually exposing individuals to feared social situations in a controlled manner, helping them build confidence and reduce avoidance behaviors.

Medication can also play a role in managing social anxiety, particularly when symptoms are severe or do not improve with therapy alone. Selective serotonin reuptake inhibitors (SSRIs) and serotonin-norepinephrine reuptake inhibitors (SNRIs) are commonly prescribed to help manage anxiety symptoms. These medications work by balancing chemicals in the brain that affect mood and anxiety levels. Individuals need to work closely with a healthcare provider to determine the most appropriate treatment plan and to monitor for any potential side effects.

Combining therapy with medication can offer a comprehensive approach to managing social anxiety disorder. Personalized treatment plans that address both the psychological and physiological aspects of the condition can help individuals achieve significant improvements in their symptoms and overall functioning.

SOCIAL SKILLS TRAINING

Social skills training is a valuable component of managing social anxiety disorder, as it helps individuals develop and refine their interpersonal skills. This type of training often involves role-playing exercises, social interaction practice, and feedback sessions to enhance confidence and competence in social settings. By practicing specific skills in a structured environment, individuals can learn to navigate social interactions more effectively and reduce their anxiety.

Training typically focuses on various aspects of social interactions, including conversation starters, non-verbal communication, and assertiveness. Participants are guided through techniques to improve their ability to engage with others, express themselves clearly, and handle social situations with greater ease. This hands-on approach helps individuals build practical skills that they can apply in real-life scenarios, gradually reducing their fear and discomfort.

Effective social skills training often involve a combination of individual and group settings. Group sessions provide opportunities for participants to practice skills with others who have similar challenges, fostering a supportive environment and allowing for real-time feedback and learning from peers.

PRACTICAL TIPS FOR DAILY LIFE

Incorporating practical tips into daily life can significantly help individuals with social anxiety manage their symptoms. One effective strategy is to set small, achievable goals for social interactions. By breaking down larger social situations into manageable steps, individuals can gradually build their confidence and reduce their anxiety. For example, starting with brief, low-pressure interactions and gradually increasing the complexity of social situations can help ease the process.

Additionally, mindfulness and relaxation techniques can be beneficial in managing anxiety symptoms. Practices such as deep breathing exercises, progressive muscle relaxation, and mindfulness meditation can help individuals stay grounded and reduce the physiological symptoms of anxiety. Incorporating these techniques into daily routines can provide a sense of calm and control, making it easier to face social situations with less fear.

Maintaining a supportive network of friends, family, or support groups can be instrumental in managing social anxiety. Sharing experiences with others who understand the challenges of social anxiety can offer comfort, encouragement, and practical advice. Engaging in activities that align with personal interests and strengths can also boost confidence and provide opportunities for positive social experiences.

CHAPTER FOUR

SPECIFIC PHOBIAS

TYPES OF PHOBIAS

Phobias are classified into specific types based on the object or situation that triggers intense fear. Common types include agoraphobia, which involves fear of being in situations where escape might be difficult, and social phobia, characterized by anxiety about social interactions and being judged by others. Specific phobias can also involve fears of particular objects or scenarios, such as heights, spiders, or flying. Each type of phobia can significantly disrupt daily life and may vary in severity from mild discomfort to debilitating anxiety.

Understanding the different types of phobias helps in identifying the appropriate treatment approaches. For instance, someone with claustrophobia, a fear of confined spaces, might avoid elevators or crowded rooms, while an individual with a fear of animals might go out of their way to avoid parks or zoos.

Recognizing these patterns is crucial for developing effective coping strategies and interventions.

Each phobia triggers a distinct pattern of avoidance and distress, necessitating tailored therapeutic interventions. Recognizing the specific type of phobia can guide individuals in seeking targeted support, such as exposure therapy for specific fears or cognitive-behavioral therapy for broader anxiety issues. Accurate identification is the first step toward effective treatment and management.

DIAGNOSTIC CRITERIA

The diagnostic criteria for phobias are outlined in the Diagnostic and Statistical Manual of Mental Disorders (DSM-5). To be diagnosed with a specific phobia, the fear must be persistent, typically lasting for six months or more, and it should cause significant distress or impairment in social, occupational, or other areas of functioning. The phobic stimulus should provoke an immediate anxiety response, such as a panic attack or intense fear, and the individual often recognizes that their fear is excessive or unreasonable.

Clinicians use structured interviews and questionnaires to assess these criteria. During the assessment, individuals may be asked about their specific fears, the frequency and intensity of their anxiety, and how it impacts their daily lives. The goal is to ensure that the symptoms align with the criteria for a specific phobia and that other mental health conditions are ruled out.

Diagnosis also involves evaluating the context of the fear. For example, a fear of flying that prevents travel and significantly impacts personal and professional life would be assessed differently from a mild discomfort experienced occasionally.

EXPOSURE THERAPY

Exposure therapy is a well-established treatment for phobias that involves gradual and systematic exposure to the feared object or situation. The process begins with creating a hierarchy of fears, starting with less anxiety-provoking scenarios and gradually working up to more challenging situations. For example, someone with a fear of flying might first look at pictures of airplanes, then watch videos, and eventually visit an airport before taking a flight.

The goal of exposure therapy is to help individuals confront their fears in a controlled and supportive environment, reducing avoidance behaviors and diminishing anxiety over time. This gradual exposure helps to desensitize the individual to the phobic stimulus, allowing them to build confidence and learn new coping strategies.

Therapists often use cognitive restructuring alongside exposure therapy to address irrational thoughts associated with the phobia. By challenging these thoughts and providing coping mechanisms, individuals can develop a more realistic and less fearful perspective of the feared object or situation.

SELF-HELP STRATEGIES

Self-help strategies are crucial for managing phobias and can complement professional treatment. Techniques such as relaxation exercises, mindfulness, and deep breathing can help individuals manage anxiety symptoms when they encounter their fears. Practicing these techniques regularly can reduce overall stress and improve emotional resilience.

Gradual exposure is another self-help strategy that involves slowly facing the feared object or situation in a controlled manner. Starting with less intimidating scenarios and gradually increasing exposure helps individuals build tolerance and confidence. Keeping a journal of progress and challenges can also be beneficial for tracking improvements and setbacks.

Seeking social support from friends, family, or support groups can provide encouragement and practical advice. Sharing experiences with others who have similar fears can offer valuable insights and coping strategies, fostering a sense of understanding and community.

REAL-LIFE EXPERIENCES

Real-life experiences of individuals with phobias illustrate the profound impact these fears can have on daily life. For example, someone with a severe fear of spiders might avoid outdoor activities, leading to social isolation and missed opportunities.

 Their journey to overcome this fear might involve exposure therapy, where they gradually interact with spiders in a controlled environment, leading to significant improvements in their quality of life.

Personal accounts often highlight the challenges and successes faced during the recovery process. Individuals might describe how confronting their fears led to unexpected positive outcomes, such as improved self-esteem or enhanced social interactions. These stories can offer hope and practical insights for others struggling with similar phobias.

Listening to and learning from others' experiences can provide valuable perspectives on managing phobias. Real-life examples can inspire and motivate those dealing with phobias to seek help and persist through the treatment process, demonstrating that overcoming these fears is achievable with the right support and strategies.

CHAPTER FIVE

OBSESSIVE-COMPULSIVE DISORDER (OCD)

DEFINITION AND SYMPTOMS

Obsessive-Compulsive Disorder (OCD) is a mental health condition characterized by persistent, intrusive thoughts (obsessions) and repetitive behaviors or mental acts (compulsions) performed to alleviate the distress caused by these thoughts. Obsessions often revolve around fears of contamination, harm, or a need for symmetry, while compulsions might include actions like excessive handwashing, checking locks, or counting.

These compulsions are meant to reduce the anxiety linked to the obsessions but often end up taking considerable time and interfering with daily functioning.

Individuals with OCD may experience symptoms that disrupt their daily lives, such as spending hours engaging in rituals or avoiding situations that trigger their obsessions. The severity of OCD can vary, with some people managing symptoms with minimal impact, while others may find that the disorder consumes much of their time and energy. Common signs include an overwhelming need to perform tasks in a specific order or an intense fear of making mistakes, leading to repeated checks and rituals.

Recognizing OCD symptoms early can help in seeking appropriate treatment. It's essential to differentiate between typical worries and the distressing, persistent thoughts that characterize OCD.

The impact of OCD extends beyond the individual, affecting relationships, work, and overall quality of life, making understanding and addressing the symptoms crucial for effective management.

COMMON OBSESSIONS AND COMPULSIONS

Common obsessions in OCD include fears of contamination, such as worries about germs or dirt, and fears of harming others, even if these thoughts are irrational. People may also experience intrusive thoughts about harming themselves or loved ones or fears of losing control. These obsessions can lead to significant distress and anxiety, compelling individuals to engage in specific behaviors to neutralize these fears.

Compulsions are the actions performed in response to obsessions, aiming to reduce the anxiety associated with intrusive thoughts.

For instance, someone with contamination fears might wash their hands repeatedly, while someone fearing harm might check locks multiple times before leaving the house. Other common compulsions include arranging objects in a precise way, counting items, or mentally repeating phrases to ward off perceived dangers.

Understanding these common obsessions and compulsions is key to recognizing OCD. The repetitive nature of these behaviors can provide temporary relief but often reinforces the cycle of anxiety and compulsion. Identifying these patterns helps in addressing the disorder through appropriate therapeutic interventions and reducing the impact on daily functioning.

TREATMENT OPTIONS

Treating OCD typically involves a combination of medication and psychotherapy. Selective serotonin reuptake inhibitors (SSRIs) are commonly prescribed to help manage the symptoms by altering brain chemistry to reduce anxiety and obsessive thoughts. These medications can be effective in alleviating the intensity of symptoms, but they often need to be taken for several weeks to show significant effects.

Psychotherapy, particularly Cognitive Behavioral Therapy (CBT), is another cornerstone of OCD treatment. CBT focuses on changing maladaptive thought patterns and behaviors.

Exposure and Response Prevention (ERP), a specific type of CBT, involves gradually exposing individuals to their fears and preventing compulsive responses, which helps reduce the anxiety associated with obsessions over time.

Combining medication with psychotherapy can offer a comprehensive approach to managing OCD. It's essential to work with healthcare professionals to tailor treatment plans to individual needs and to monitor progress regularly. Effective treatment not only alleviates symptoms but also improves overall quality of life by helping individuals regain control over their thoughts and behaviors.

COGNITIVE BEHAVIORAL THERAPY (CBT) FOR OCD

Cognitive Behavioral Therapy (CBT) is a widely used and effective approach for treating OCD. The therapy aims to change the dysfunctional thought patterns that drive obsessive fears and compulsive behaviors. Through CBT, individuals learn to recognize and challenge irrational beliefs and replace them with more balanced and realistic thoughts.

Exposure and Response Prevention (ERP) is a key component of CBT for OCD. This technique involves exposing individuals to the sources of their anxiety (exposure) while encouraging them to refrain from performing their usual compulsive responses (response prevention). Over time, ERP helps reduce the power of obsessions and the urge to engage in compulsions by breaking the cycle of reinforcement.

CBT for OCD requires active participation from the individual, including practicing new skills outside of therapy sessions. The therapy can be intensive but is often highly effective in helping individuals manage their symptoms and improve their daily functioning. Support from a trained therapist is crucial in guiding the process and ensuring the therapy is tailored to each person's specific needs.

PERSONAL STORIES AND EXAMPLES

Personal stories and examples of individuals with OCD can provide valuable insights into the lived experience of the disorder.

Many people with OCD have shared their journeys of overcoming challenges, detailing their struggles with intrusive thoughts and their impact on their daily lives. These stories often highlight the intensity of obsessions and the lengths to which individuals go to manage their compulsions.

For example, one individual might describe their battle with a fear of contamination, leading to excessive handwashing and rituals that consume hours of their day.

Others might share their experience with intrusive thoughts about harming others, leading to repetitive checking and reassurance-seeking. Such personal accounts can illustrate the diverse ways OCD manifests and the profound effect it has on personal and professional life.

Hearing these stories can be both enlightening and comforting for those struggling with similar issues, offering hope and demonstrating that effective treatment and management strategies are available. Personal experiences also underscore the importance of empathy and understanding for those dealing with OCD, fostering a supportive environment for recovery and self-acceptance.

CHAPTER SIX

CAUSES AND RISK FACTORS

GENETIC AND BIOLOGICAL FACTORS

Genetic and biological factors play a significant role in the development of anxiety disorders. Research has shown that anxiety can run in families, suggesting a hereditary component. Genetic predispositions involve variations in genes that affect brain chemistry and stress response systems. For instance, alterations in neurotransmitter systems, such as serotonin and gamma-aminobutyric acid (GABA), can make individuals more susceptible to anxiety. If a close relative has an anxiety disorder, the likelihood of developing similar symptoms increases, indicating a genetic link.

Biological factors also include the functioning of brain structures involved in fear and stress regulation. The amygdala, responsible for processing emotions, and the prefrontal cortex, which helps regulate these emotions, can both influence anxiety levels. Dysregulation in these areas might contribute to heightened anxiety responses. Additionally, hormonal imbalances, such as those involving cortisol, a stress hormone, can affect how the body responds to stressors, further influencing the likelihood of developing an anxiety disorder.

Understanding these factors can help in identifying individuals at risk and tailoring preventive and therapeutic strategies. Genetic counseling might be beneficial for those with a family history of anxiety disorders, while biological assessments can aid in creating personalized treatment plans. Interventions often focus on balancing neurotransmitters and addressing hormonal imbalances through medication or lifestyle adjustments.

ENVIRONMENTAL INFLUENCES

Environmental influences encompass a range of external factors that can contribute to the development of anxiety disorders.

Early life experiences, such as parental stress, childhood trauma, or exposure to a chaotic home environment, can significantly impact emotional regulation and stress response systems. For example, children raised in high-stress households may develop heightened anxiety due to constant exposure to conflict or instability.

Moreover, life events such as losing a loved one, experiencing abuse, or undergoing significant life changes like moving or changing schools can act as triggers for anxiety. These events often overwhelm an individual's coping mechanisms, leading to the onset or exacerbation of anxiety disorders. Social factors, such as peer pressure or bullying, can also contribute to developing anxiety, particularly in adolescents.

Addressing environmental influences involves creating supportive and stable environments. Interventions might include therapy that focuses on processing past trauma, building resilience, and developing healthy coping strategies. Support systems, including family counseling and community support groups, can provide the necessary environment to mitigate the effects of adverse experiences.

PSYCHOLOGICAL FACTORS

Psychological factors include cognitive patterns and personality traits that contribute to the development of anxiety disorders. Individuals with certain cognitive distortions, such as catastrophizing or overgeneralizing, may be more prone to anxiety. These patterns involve interpreting situations in the worst possible light, which can exacerbate feelings of fear and worry. Cognitive-behavioral therapy (CBT) is often used to address these distortions by helping individuals reframe their thoughts and develop healthier thinking patterns.

Additionally, personality traits such as high neuroticism, characterized by a tendency to experience negative emotions, can increase vulnerability to anxiety. People with this trait may react more intensely to stressors and perceive situations as more threatening. Understanding these traits allows for targeted therapeutic approaches that focus on modifying maladaptive thought processes and enhancing emotional regulation skills.

Psychological factors can be addressed through various therapeutic techniques. CBT, for example, helps individuals recognize and alter irrational thoughts and beliefs that contribute to anxiety. Therapeutic interventions also focus on building self-esteem, improving self-efficacy, and developing effective coping strategies to manage stress and anxiety.

STRESS AND TRAUMA

Stress and trauma are significant contributors to anxiety disorders, often acting as catalysts for their development. Prolonged exposure to stress, whether from work, relationships, or financial problems, can overwhelm the body's ability to cope, leading to persistent anxiety. Acute traumatic events, such as accidents, assaults, or natural disasters, can also trigger anxiety disorders, particularly post-traumatic stress disorder (PTSD). The symptoms of PTSD include flashbacks, nightmares, and severe anxiety related to the traumatic event.

Traumatic experiences can cause changes in brain function and stress hormone levels, which affect how individuals process and respond to stress. Over time, these changes can lead to a heightened state of anxiety and difficulty managing stress. It is crucial to address trauma and stress through therapeutic methods that focus on processing the traumatic experience and developing effective coping mechanisms.

Treatment for stress and trauma-related anxiety often includes trauma-focused therapies, such as Eye Movement Desensitization and Reprocessing (EMDR) or trauma-focused CBT. These therapies help individuals process and integrate traumatic experiences, reducing their impact on daily functioning. Additionally, stress management techniques, such as mindfulness and relaxation exercises, can aid in reducing overall anxiety and improving coping strategies.

PREVENTIVE MEASURES

Preventive measures for anxiety disorders involve strategies aimed at reducing risk factors and promoting mental well-being. Building resilience through lifestyle changes and healthy coping mechanisms can play a crucial role in preventing anxiety.

Regular physical exercise, a balanced diet, and sufficient sleep are foundational elements that contribute to overall mental health and stress management. Engaging in activities that promote relaxation, such as mindfulness meditation or yoga, can also help manage stress levels and prevent the onset of anxiety disorders.

Education and awareness about anxiety and its symptoms are vital for early intervention. Individuals who understand the signs of anxiety are more likely to seek help before their condition worsens. Preventive measures also include building strong social support networks, which provide emotional support and reduce feelings of isolation. Support from friends, family, or support groups can be instrumental in managing stress and maintaining mental health.

Early intervention and regular mental health check-ups can prevent the escalation of anxiety symptoms. Professional guidance, such as counseling or therapy, can offer personalized strategies to manage stress and anxiety effectively. By integrating these preventive measures into daily life, individuals can maintain mental well-being and reduce their risk of developing anxiety disorders.

CHAPTER SEVEN
DIAGNOSIS AND ASSESSMENT
DIAGNOSTIC TOOLS AND TECHNIQUES

Diagnosis of anxiety disorders involves various tools and techniques that help professionals assess the severity and type of anxiety a person may be experiencing.

Common diagnostic tools include structured interviews, such as the Anxiety and Depression Association of America (ADAA) guidelines and the Generalized Anxiety Disorder 7 (GAD-7) scale. These tools provide a standardized approach to assessing symptoms, helping clinicians identify patterns and severity. Additionally, self-report questionnaires and symptom checklists offer valuable insights into an individual's experience of anxiety, providing a detailed picture of their condition.

Psychological assessments often involve combining these tools with behavioral observations and clinical interviews. For instance, clinicians may use the Hamilton Anxiety Rating Scale (HAM-A) to gauge the level of anxiety experienced by the patient and observe how anxiety affects their daily functioning. These assessments help in differentiating between various types of anxiety disorders, such as generalized anxiety disorder, social anxiety disorder, and panic disorder, ensuring that the diagnosis is as accurate as possible.

In some cases, diagnostic tools are complemented by physiological measurements, like heart rate variability or cortisol levels, to understand the physiological impact of anxiety. This multimodal approach allows for a comprehensive evaluation, integrating both subjective reports and objective data, to create a well-rounded picture of the individual's anxiety profile.

ROLE OF MENTAL HEALTH PROFESSIONALS

Mental health professionals, including psychologists, psychiatrists, and licensed clinical social workers, play a crucial role in diagnosing and treating anxiety disorders. These professionals are trained to use diagnostic tools and techniques effectively, providing accurate assessments based on established criteria. They also offer therapeutic interventions tailored to the individual's needs, such as cognitive-behavioral therapy (CBT) or medication management.

Psychologists often conduct in-depth clinical interviews and administer psychological tests to identify the presence of anxiety disorders and their impact on the individual's functioning.

Psychiatrists may evaluate the need for medication and provide pharmacological treatments to help manage symptoms. Clinical social workers often offer supportive counseling and assist with accessing community resources.

Additionally, mental health professionals work collaboratively with other healthcare providers to ensure a holistic approach to treatment. They may coordinate with primary care physicians, occupational therapists, or nutritionists to address various aspects of the individual's health, ensuring comprehensive care and support throughout the treatment process.

SELF-DIAGNOSIS RISKS

Self-diagnosis of anxiety disorders poses significant risks, as it can lead to misinterpretation of symptoms and inappropriate treatment approaches. Individuals who attempt to diagnose themselves may overlook critical factors that a trained professional would identify, such as co-occurring conditions or underlying medical issues.

This can result in a misunderstanding of the severity or nature of their anxiety, potentially leading to inadequate or harmful self-treatment methods.

Self-diagnosis also lacks the benefit of clinical validation, which ensures that the diagnosis is accurate and reliable. Without professional oversight, individuals may use online resources or self-help tools that provide generic or inaccurate information, leading to misguided self-care practices. This can exacerbate anxiety symptoms or delay effective treatment, causing further distress.

Moreover, self-diagnosis can contribute to stigma and mental health misconceptions. Individuals who diagnose themselves may feel isolated or judged, impacting their willingness to seek professional help. Proper diagnosis by a mental health professional helps reduce stigma and encourages a supportive and informed approach to managing anxiety disorders.

IMPORTANCE OF ACCURATE ASSESSMENT

Accurate assessment of anxiety disorders is crucial for effective treatment and management. A precise diagnosis allows mental health professionals to develop tailored treatment plans that address the specific needs of the individual.

It ensures that the chosen interventions, whether therapeutic or pharmacological, are appropriate and targeted, improving the likelihood of successful outcomes.

An accurate assessment also helps in distinguishing between different types of anxiety disorders and ruling out other conditions that may present with similar symptoms.

For example, differentiating between panic disorder and social anxiety disorder is essential for selecting the correct treatment approach. Accurate assessments provide a clear understanding of the individual's condition, allowing for more focused and effective therapeutic strategies.

Additionally, accurate assessment facilitates monitoring progress over time. By establishing a baseline and regularly evaluating changes in symptoms, mental health professionals can adjust treatment plans as needed. This dynamic approach ensures that the treatment remains effective and responsive to the individual's evolving needs, promoting better long-term management of anxiety.

CASE STUDIES

Case studies provide valuable insights into the application of diagnostic tools and techniques in real-world scenarios. They illustrate how different anxiety disorders present in individuals and how professionals use various assessments to achieve accurate diagnoses. For instance, a case study might detail a patient's experience with generalized anxiety disorder, including their symptoms, the diagnostic process, and the resulting treatment plan.

These case studies often highlight the role of mental health professionals in diagnosing and treating anxiety disorders, showcasing their approach to assessment and intervention. They can also demonstrate the risks associated with self-diagnosis, showing how professional input is essential for an accurate understanding of the individual's condition.

Furthermore, case studies offer examples of how accurate assessments lead to successful treatment outcomes.

By reviewing real-life examples, individuals can better understand the practical application of diagnostic tools and techniques, the importance of professional evaluation, and the benefits of a well-informed approach to managing anxiety disorders.

CHAPTER EIGHT

TREATMENT APPROACHES

COGNITIVE BEHAVIORAL THERAPY (CBT)

Cognitive Behavioral Therapy (CBT) is a widely recognized approach for treating anxiety disorders by focusing on changing negative thought patterns and behaviors. In CBT, patients work with therapists to identify and challenge distorted thinking, learning to replace harmful beliefs with more realistic ones. For instance, a person with social anxiety may learn to reframe thoughts about social interactions, shifting from fearing judgment to understanding that most social situations are neutral or positive.

Practically, CBT often involves exposure exercises where individuals gradually face feared situations in a controlled manner. This technique helps to desensitize them to their anxiety triggers. Patients might start with less intimidating scenarios and progressively confront more challenging ones. Through this method, they learn that their feared outcomes are often less severe than anticipated, which reduces overall anxiety.

The therapy also includes skill-building exercises such as relaxation techniques and problem-solving strategies. Patients are taught how to manage anxiety symptoms in real time by employing these skills. For example, breathing exercises or progressive muscle relaxation can help mitigate anxiety during stressful situations, aiding in overall symptom control.

MEDICATION OPTIONS

Medication options for anxiety disorders are typically considered when symptoms are severe or do not improve with therapy alone. Antidepressants, particularly selective serotonin reuptake inhibitors (SSRIs), are commonly prescribed to manage anxiety. These medications work by increasing levels of serotonin in the brain, which can help stabilize mood and reduce anxiety.

For example, medications like sertraline or escitalopram are often used to treat generalized anxiety disorder.

Additionally, benzodiazepines may be prescribed for short-term relief of acute anxiety symptoms due to their fast-acting properties. However, due to the risk of dependency, these are generally used only for brief periods or in specific situations. Medications like diazepam or lorazepam can provide quick relief but should be managed carefully under the guidance of a healthcare provider.

Antianxiety medications might also include beta-blockers for physical symptoms of anxiety, such as rapid heartbeat. These medications can help reduce the physiological effects of anxiety, making them useful for individuals who experience significant physical symptoms in stressful situations. Each medication type has its benefits and potential side effects, so ongoing consultation with a healthcare provider is essential to tailor treatment to the individual's needs.

LIFESTYLE ADJUSTMENTS

Lifestyle adjustments play a crucial role in managing anxiety disorders and complement other treatment methods. Regular physical activity, such as walking, running, or yoga, has been shown to reduce anxiety levels by promoting the release of endorphins and improving overall mood. Engaging in exercise routines can also provide a structured outlet for stress and improve sleep patterns, which can further alleviate anxiety.

Diet and nutrition also impact anxiety levels. Maintaining a balanced diet rich in fruits, vegetables, lean proteins, and whole grains supports overall health and can affect mood regulation. Avoiding excessive caffeine, alcohol, and sugar can help reduce anxiety symptoms, as these substances can exacerbate feelings of nervousness or tension.

Additionally, establishing a consistent sleep routine is vital for managing anxiety. Poor sleep can heighten anxiety symptoms, while adequate rest helps regulate mood and stress levels. Implementing good sleep hygiene practices, such as maintaining a regular sleep schedule and creating a relaxing bedtime routine, can contribute to improved mental health and reduced anxiety.

COMPLEMENTARY THERAPIES

Complementary therapies, such as mindfulness and acupuncture, can support traditional treatments for anxiety disorders. Mindfulness practices, including meditation and deep breathing exercises, help individuals stay present and reduce excessive worry. By focusing on the current moment and observing thoughts without judgment, individuals can decrease anxiety and improve emotional regulation.

Acupuncture, a traditional Chinese medicine technique, involves inserting thin needles into specific points on the body to balance energy flow. Some studies suggest that acupuncture can help reduce anxiety symptoms by promoting relaxation and influencing neurotransmitter activity.

Patients often report feeling more calm and balanced after sessions, which can complement other anxiety treatments.

Additionally, practices like aromatherapy and massage therapy can provide relaxation and stress relief. Essential oils such as lavender and chamomile have calming effects, while massage therapy can reduce muscle tension and promote overall relaxation. Integrating these therapies into a comprehensive treatment plan can enhance well-being and support the management of anxiety symptoms.

MANAGING TREATMENT PROGRESS

Managing treatment progress involves regularly assessing and adjusting therapeutic approaches based on the individual's response. This includes scheduling follow-up appointments with therapists or healthcare providers to evaluate the effectiveness of treatments and make necessary adjustments. For example, if a particular medication is not yielding the desired results, a provider may recommend changes in dosage or try alternative medications.

Tracking symptoms and progress through journaling or using anxiety scales can provide valuable insights into how well treatments are working. Individuals might record their anxiety levels, triggers, and responses to different interventions, which helps both them and their healthcare providers understand patterns and make informed decisions about treatment modifications.

It's also important to address any side effects or challenges that arise during treatment. Open communication with healthcare providers about these issues allows for timely adjustments and ensures that the treatment plan remains effective and manageable. Regular reviews and proactive adjustments to the treatment strategy are crucial for achieving and maintaining optimal outcomes in anxiety management.

CHAPTER NINE

COPING STRATEGIES AND SELF-HELP

DAILY COPING TECHNIQUES

Daily coping techniques are essential for managing anxiety disorders and improving overall well-being. One effective approach is to establish a structured routine that includes regular sleep, balanced meals, and physical activity. By setting a consistent daily schedule, individuals can create a sense of stability and predictability that reduces anxiety. Incorporating simple practices such as journaling, where you write down your thoughts and feelings, can also help in processing emotions and identifying patterns that contribute to anxiety. Additionally, integrating brief moments of relaxation throughout the day, such as taking short breaks for deep breathing exercises, can help manage stress levels and keep anxiety in check.

Another practical coping technique involves using cognitive-behavioral strategies to challenge and reframe negative thought patterns. This can be done through thought-stopping exercises, where you consciously interrupt and replace negative thoughts with more positive or realistic alternatives. Engaging in activities that provide a sense of achievement or pleasure, such as hobbies or creative projects, can also be beneficial.

These activities serve as distractions from anxiety and promote a more positive outlook. Regular self-monitoring and adjusting these techniques based on personal effectiveness can lead to improved management of anxiety.

Incorporating relaxation techniques into daily routines can further enhance coping strategies. Techniques such as progressive muscle relaxation, where you systematically tense and then relax different muscle groups, can reduce physical symptoms of anxiety.

Using guided imagery or visualization exercises, where you imagine yourself in a calming environment, can also be effective. Integrating these practices into your daily routine helps in creating a toolkit of strategies that can be used whenever anxiety arises, promoting a more balanced and manageable response to stress.

BUILDING RESILIENCE

Building resilience is a crucial component of managing anxiety disorders effectively. Resilience involves developing the ability to bounce back from stress and adversity, and it can be cultivated through various strategies.

One approach is to focus on strengthening problem-solving skills, which helps individuals handle challenges more effectively. By breaking down problems into manageable steps and setting achievable goals, individuals can build confidence in their ability to navigate difficult situations. Reflecting on past successes and recognizing personal strengths also contribute to greater resilience.

Emotional regulation is another key aspect of resilience. Learning to identify and understand your emotions, as well as practicing techniques for managing them, can improve your ability to cope with stress.

Strategies such as emotional journaling, where you record and analyze your emotional experiences, can help you develop greater self-awareness and control. Additionally, developing a positive mindset and maintaining optimism can enhance resilience by encouraging a focus on growth and solutions rather than obstacles.

Social support plays a significant role in building resilience. Connecting with friends, family, or support groups provides a network of individuals who can offer encouragement, advice, and understanding. Building and maintaining these relationships can create a sense of belonging and provide practical help during challenging times.

Engaging in activities that foster social connections, such as volunteering or joining community groups, can also enhance your support system and contribute to greater resilience.

MINDFULNESS AND RELAXATION EXERCISES

Mindfulness and relaxation exercises are valuable tools for managing anxiety disorders and promoting mental well-being. Mindfulness involves paying attention to the present moment without judgment, which helps reduce rumination and stress.

One effective mindfulness practice is mindfulness meditation, where you sit quietly and focus on your breath, observing any thoughts or sensations that arise without becoming attached to them. This practice helps in developing a non-reactive awareness that can reduce anxiety and improve overall emotional regulation.

Relaxation exercises, such as deep breathing techniques, are also beneficial in managing anxiety.

Deep breathing involves taking slow, deep breaths from the diaphragm, which can help activate the body's relaxation response and reduce physiological symptoms of anxiety. Progressive muscle relaxation, where you tense and then relax different muscle groups, can help alleviate physical tension associated with anxiety. Regular practice of these techniques can lead to increased relaxation and decreased stress levels over time.

Incorporating mindfulness and relaxation practices into your daily routine can enhance their effectiveness. Setting aside specific times each day for mindfulness exercises or relaxation techniques helps create a consistent practice that becomes part of your routine.

Using apps or guided recordings can also provide support and structure for your practice. By regularly engaging in these exercises, you can develop a greater sense of calm and better manage anxiety symptoms.

SUPPORT SYSTEMS AND RESOURCES

Support systems and resources are crucial for effectively managing anxiety disorders. Building a network of supportive individuals, such as friends, family members, or mental health professionals, provides emotional and practical assistance during times of stress.

Reaching out for support can include sharing your experiences with others who understand or seeking advice from those who have experienced similar challenges. Building strong, positive relationships and communicating openly about your needs can create a reliable support system.

In addition to personal support, accessing professional resources can significantly aid in managing anxiety. Therapists or counselors trained in cognitive-behavioral therapy (CBT) or other evidence-based approaches can provide valuable guidance and strategies for coping with anxiety.

Support groups, both in-person and online, offer a platform for connecting with others who face similar issues, sharing experiences, and gaining insights. Utilizing these resources can enhance your understanding of anxiety and provide additional tools for managing symptoms.

Educational resources, such as self-help books, online courses, or workshops, can also be beneficial. These resources offer practical advice, coping strategies, and information on anxiety management. Engaging with educational materials can empower you with knowledge and skills to better handle anxiety. Combining personal support, professional help, and educational resources creates a comprehensive approach to managing anxiety and improving overall mental health.

LONG-TERM STRATEGIES FOR MANAGEMENT

Long-term strategies for managing anxiety disorders focus on creating sustainable practices that promote ongoing mental health and well-being.

Establishing a consistent self-care routine is fundamental, including regular physical activity, a balanced diet, and adequate sleep. These practices support overall health and contribute to better management of anxiety symptoms. Setting long-term goals, such as developing coping skills or pursuing personal interests can provide direction and motivation in managing anxiety.

Engaging in continuous learning and personal development is also important for long-term anxiety management. This can involve participating in therapy or counseling, attending workshops, or exploring new relaxation techniques. By staying informed about new strategies and maintaining a proactive approach to mental health, individuals can adapt to changing needs and challenges. Developing resilience through ongoing personal growth helps in managing anxiety more effectively over time.

Maintaining and nurturing support systems is crucial for long-term success. Regularly connecting with friends, family, or support groups ensures a continued network of support. Additionally, practicing self-reflection and adapting coping strategies as needed can help in addressing new or evolving challenges. By integrating these long-term strategies into daily life, individuals can create a stable foundation for managing anxiety and enhancing overall well-being.

CHAPTER TEN

COMMON CONCERNS AND FAQS

WHAT ARE THE MOST COMMON SIGNS OF ANXIETY DISORDERS?

Anxiety disorders often manifest through persistent and excessive worry that is difficult to control. Individuals might experience intense fear or apprehension about everyday situations, even when there is no imminent danger. Physical symptoms such as rapid heartbeat, sweating, and muscle tension are frequently observed.

These signs can lead to noticeable distress and disruptions in daily activities, impacting the overall quality of life.

Behavioral changes are also common, including avoidance of situations that trigger anxiety. People with anxiety disorders may avoid social gatherings, public speaking, or even everyday tasks, which can lead to isolation.

This avoidance behavior often exacerbates feelings of anxiety and contributes to a cycle of fear and retreat from situations that could otherwise be manageable.

Cognitive symptoms can include persistent negative thoughts, excessive rumination, and an inability to relax. This constant mental stress can lead to difficulty concentrating, memory problems, and a general feeling of being overwhelmed. Recognizing these symptoms is crucial for identifying whether anxiety may be crossing into a disorder rather than just temporary stress.

HOW CAN I DIFFERENTIATE BETWEEN NORMAL ANXIETY AND AN ANXIETY DISORDER?

Normal anxiety is typically a reaction to specific stressors or challenging situations and usually diminishes once the situation is resolved or the stressor is removed. In contrast, an anxiety disorder is characterized by persistent and intense anxiety that occurs without a clear reason or continues even after the stressor is gone.

It often interferes with daily functioning and quality of life, extending beyond occasional bouts of worry or stress.

The duration and intensity of anxiety symptoms are key differentiators. While normal anxiety might last for a short period and fluctuate with circumstances, anxiety disorders involve chronic and debilitating symptoms that persist for six months or longer. These symptoms are often disproportionate to the actual threat or stressor and can significantly impair one's ability to perform routine tasks.

Physical and emotional symptoms in anxiety disorders are more severe and can escalate over time. Individuals might experience frequent panic attacks, severe avoidance behaviors, and persistent feelings of dread. Seeking professional assessment can help in distinguishing between normal anxiety and an anxiety disorder by evaluating the frequency, duration, and impact of the symptoms on one's life.

WHAT ARE THE FIRST STEPS IF I THINK I HAVE AN ANXIETY DISORDER?

The initial step is to consult a healthcare professional, such as a primary care physician or mental health specialist. They can conduct a thorough assessment to determine if an anxiety disorder is present.

This evaluation often includes discussing symptoms, their impact on daily life, and any underlying medical or psychological conditions that could be contributing to the anxiety.

After a diagnosis is made, the healthcare provider will discuss treatment options, which may include therapy, medication, or a combination of both. Cognitive-behavioral therapy (CBT) is commonly recommended as it helps individuals identify and change negative thought patterns and behaviors associated with anxiety. Medication options might include antidepressants or anti-anxiety medications to manage symptoms.

It's also important to develop a support system by connecting with friends, family, or support groups. Engaging in open discussions about your anxiety can provide emotional support and practical advice from those who understand what you're going through. Building a supportive environment is crucial for managing and reducing anxiety symptoms effectively.

HOW LONG DOES TREATMENT TYPICALLY TAKE?

The duration of treatment for anxiety disorders varies depending on the individual and the severity of their symptoms. Typically, therapy such as cognitive-behavioral therapy (CBT) can last between 12 to 20 weeks, though some people may benefit from longer-term therapy. The focus is on teaching coping mechanisms and helping individuals manage their anxiety more effectively over time.

Medication, if prescribed, may take several weeks to show noticeable effects. The duration of medication use varies; some individuals may need to continue taking medication for an extended period, while others may use it only temporarily during acute phases. Regular follow-ups with a healthcare provider are essential to adjust dosages and assess the effectiveness of the medication.

Ongoing treatment might involve periodic check-ins with a therapist or counselor to address any residual or recurring symptoms. Even after the initial treatment phase, continued self-care and coping strategies are crucial for maintaining progress and managing anxiety in the long term.

WHAT ARE SOME EFFECTIVE SELF-HELP STRATEGIES FOR MANAGING ANXIETY?

Developing a routine that includes regular physical exercise can significantly reduce anxiety. Activities such as walking, jogging, or yoga help to release endorphins, which are natural mood lifters.

Incorporating relaxation techniques, such as deep breathing exercises and progressive muscle relaxation, can also help to calm the mind and reduce physical symptoms of anxiety.

Maintaining a healthy lifestyle by eating a balanced diet, getting adequate sleep, and avoiding excessive caffeine or alcohol can positively impact anxiety levels. Setting small, achievable goals and practicing mindfulness or meditation can help manage stress and improve overall emotional well-being. Keeping a journal to track anxiety triggers and progress can also provide valuable insights and help in developing coping strategies.

Building and nurturing a support network is vital for managing anxiety. Engaging with friends, family, or support groups can provide emotional support and practical advice. Additionally, seeking educational resources or workshops on anxiety management can offer new tools and techniques for handling anxiety in daily life.